RUSSIAN ICONS

From the 12th to the 15th Century

FONTANA UNESCO ART BOOKS

Egyptian Wall-Paintings
Spanish Frescoes
Persian Miniatures
Russian Icons

Russian Icons

FROM THE 12th TO THE 15th CENTURY

Victor Lasareff

COLLINS · UNESCO

Russian icons are an important part of mediaeval painting. Their aesthetic value, however, was not fully realized until exhibitions of early icons began to be held. The first, the Russian Mediaeval Art Exhibition, took place in 1913 in Moscow. It struck the public by the breathtaking beauty of an art whose charm resides in pure and spontaneous feeling, harmonious composition and extraordinarily eloquent figures. The interplay of colours was unparalleled in luminosity and gaiety by anything in Byzantine, Roman or Gothic art.

It is only when they have been cleaned of dark varnishes and repainting that the Russian primitives appear in their true light. But this fact was not always recognized by collectors, or even by museums, for they did not really know the treasures in their possession. Partially hidden by metal frames and several coats of paint, the Russian icons looked dull and dreary. They took on a new lease of life towards the end of the XIXth century when they were systematically cleaned of retouches and varnishes. Then the darkened and obscured colours shone radiantly as new. The long, painstaking work of the restorers revealed hundreds of icons which are the pride of the Russian Museum, Leningrad, the Tretyakov Gallery, Moscow, and the Art and History Museum, Novgorod. It is a matter for regret that icons are not very well represented in western museums, which possess only unimportant works.

St. George. Novgorod School. Circa 1770. Cathedral of the Annunciation, Kremlin, Moscow.

The Saviour in Glory, by Andrei Rublëv. Circa 1420.
Tretyakov Gallery, Moscow.

To have a true conception of early Russian painting one must visit the museums of the USSR.

We have no example of Slav painting of the pre-Christian period. However, early chronicles allude to pagan temples built of wood and decorated with paintings. When Russia was converted to Christianity under the grand-dukes of Kiev, around 989, many stone churches were built. The Russians, like the Byzantines, decorated their churches with frescoes, mosaics and icons. We know that Prince Vladimir employed Byzantine master masons to direct the building of the Dessiatinnaya Church at Kiev (989-996). Byzantine master masons also collaborated in the building of the great cathedral of St. Sophia at Kiev (1037-1046) during the reign of Yaroslav, son of Vladimir. As elsewhere in mediaeval Europe, workshops of experienced artists were entrusted with important buildings. At first the painters brought from Constantinople took charge, with Russian artists as their assistants and pupils. However, the local painters gradually replaced their masters and the Greco-Russian workshops became purely Russian. In this way a Russian school of architecture and a Russian school of painting came into being.

The earliest Russian icons are the Novgorod ones. In the xiith century, with the decay of the Kiev duchy, Novgorod obtained its independence, the power of the princes weakened and a republican form of government was set up. Later on, the *boyars* got the upper hand, but they had to reckon with the guilds, which produced the leaders of all the municipal movements.

It was in the xiith century that Novgorod art achieved its individuality. Easel painting was strongly influenced by the Byzantines, who were much in favour with the princes. This trend was to die out in the following century, but it is apparent in two remarkable icons, *Saint George* and the *Archangel* (Pl. 1). The former was painted around 1170 and is now in the Annunciation in the Kremlin. It was probably commissioned by Prince

George of Novgorod, the youngest son of Andrei Bogo-
liubsky. *Saint George,* the prince's patron saint, is represented as the guardian of the prince's arms, though the left
hand bearing the sword is only partially visible. His
powerful torso, which occupies almost the entire surface
of the panel, stands out conspicuously against a gold background. The architectural design of this open, youthful
face with its courageous expression is quite fascinating.

The *Archangel* (Pl. 1), like *St. George,* dates from the end
of the XIIth century. It belonged to the "deisis", or group
of heads which decorated the architrave of an iconostasis.
The ethereal expression of the face and the character-
istically soft treatment of light and shade relate this icon
to XIIth century works belonging indisputably to the Novgorod school, such as the Ustyug *Annunciation* and the
Saviour (Tretyakov Gallery, Moscow).

The large icon of the *Dormition* (Pl. 2) is a case on its
own. Painted at the beginning of the XIIIth century, it is
in many ways similar to the icons in the Byzantine style,
but for the first time the figures lose their relief, bright
variegated colours are used for the garments and facial
expressions are more natural. The Assumption is represented in complex iconographic form: Christ is shown
holding in his arms a child in a white robe symbolizing
the soul of the Virgin Mary which he is about to raise
to heaven. The twelve apostles are seen descending from
the skies to bow down before the Virgin's death bed, as
in the apocryphal legend. Just above the figure of Christ
four graceful angels hover against a gold ground. The
painter's aim in so placing the angels and apostles was
obviously that of all the medieval Russian masters: to
center the composition and give it a flat, decorative ap-
pearance.

Aside from Kiev and Novgorod, local schools of painting
sprang up in the XIIth century at Vladimir, Suzdal, Yaroslav and Pskov. It is to the Yaroslav school, which
flourished in the first third of the XIIIth century, that we

9

The Nativity of the Virgin. Suzdal School. Late fourteenth century. Russian Museum, Leningrad.

St. Cyril of Belozersk. School of Dionisii. 1490-1500.
Russian Museum, Leningrad.

owe the magnificent *Virgo orans* (Pl. 3). As in the famous icon from the Blachernes Church, Constantinople, the Infant Jesus is depicted, arms outstretched, in a medallion on the Virgin's breast, but the Russian version of this theme is considerably less severe. The style is bold and dynamic, the gold bands gain in width and are used to good decorative effect. At Yaroslav the dark Byzantine palette was superseded by brighter and brighter colours.

While the xiiith century witnessed the development of urban civilization in Western Europe, it was a terrible period for Russia. In 1223 the Mongol invasions began devastating the cities, and relations with Byzantium and the Balkans were broken off. Within Russia itself the provinces were more and more isolated from one another. It was no time for new building and indeed both money and labor were lacking. But the Tartars did not succeed in conquering Novgorod and Pskov and in these two privileged cities the traditions were kept alive.

The Novgorod school reached the height of its development at the turn of the xivth century and during the xvth, when its finest works were produced. With the disappearance of Byzantine influence its strong national characteristics acquired a regional flavour. Decidedly democratic, Novgorod art bears the imprint of popular taste: expressive and concise, it avoids the excessive symbolism so much in vogue with icon painters at a later date. Its themes are simple and require no commentary. Many icons were devoted to the patron saints of the peasant, for instance, the *Prophet Elijah* (Pl. 6), whom the people revered as the "Thunderer", or rainbearer, and the protector of their homes. The masters of the Novgorod school generally placed him against a background of flaming vermilion and gave him a penetrating expression. *Saint George* (Pls. 5 and 11) was also regarded as a protector of peasants, a guardian of the herds and the embodiment of the forces of light. The wise St. Nicholas was the object of a special cult: sick persons and travellers addressed their prayers to him and he was asked to intercede in cases of fire — the terrible scourge of cities and villages built of wood. The Novgorod workshops also put out icons of *St. Frol* and *St. Lavr* (Pl. 12), the protectors of horses. All these images were moving in their simplicity. And even when the Novgorod painters introduced several figures in the same icon (Pls. 4, 7, 8, 9) their compositions were always so clear and airy that they can be understood without effort, the secondary episodes never obscuring the main theme.

The artists of Novgorod liked to paint strong, vigorous types; they preferred faces with well marked national traits and even with coarse features. The figures seem an integral part of the composition as a whole. The Novgorod masters' palette consisted solely of unmixed colours, intense and remarkably vibrant tones with flaming vermilion predominating. It was not so harmonious as that of the Moscow masters; on the other hand it possessed a virile and dynamic quality all its own. Matisse admired these colours with their unforgettable brilliance and chromatic tension. In them the artistc taste of the Novgorod school is most completely expressed.

Twentieth century research produced evidence of other regional schools beside Novgorod in the xivth and xvth centuries — Tver, Pskov, Suzdal, Rostov, and even distant Kargopol near Arkangelsk. From Kargopol we have a number of remarkable icons (Pls. 13, 14, 15, 16) which once formed a part of the iconostasis of that city's cathedral. They are characteristic of what is called the "northern school", largely influenced by that of Novgorod but with a certain concise style. For instance, figures are stylized in the extreme, gestures are restrained, movements slow and elements such as hills or buildings are suggested by simple masses. These icons are the work of a great painter and an excellent colourist. The purity and tension of the colours bring to mind the Novgorod masters, but the Kargopol masters were original in that they used larger

13

The meeting of Aleksei and the Khan. Detail from hagiographical icon "The Metropolitan Aleksei". (See Plate 27).

14

St. Paraskeve (?), St. Gregory of Nazianzus and St. John Chrysostom.
Pskov School. Late fourteenth century. Tretyakov Gallery, Moscow.

15

patches of colour, avoiding unnecessary intersections and distracting effects. In that way the colouring became more vibrant, especially in areas illuminated by vermilion.

The Pskov painters used a very different colour range in which intense green and orange-red predominated. The plain, simple faces of the Pskov icons are strikingly alive. Dead white, they are modelled by means of light and shade effects and glow with an intense inner life.

The beautiful icon of the *Dormition* (Pl. 17) is attributed to the school of Tver. The apostles and saints bowing down before the Virgin form a rhythmic parabola, echoed by the parabola of the blue aura around Christ. The soul of Mary is symbolized by the child in immaculate white which Christ holds in his arms. On the clouds are repeated the busts of the apostles which appeared on the XIIIth century icon from Novgorod (Pl. 2). In the central medallion the Mother of God, before ascending to Heaven, is handing her red belt to the Apostle Thomas, who has just arrived. This theme, taken from apocryphal writings of the Vth century, is known in Italian art as "La Madonna della Cintola". It was introduced into Russia in about 1313 in the wall paintings of Snetogorski monastery. The icon of the *Dormition* is remarkable not only because of the complexity of its composition, but also because of the exceptional beauty of its colours, amongst which vibrant blues are dominant. It is known as the "Blue Assumption". Rather pale delicate colours with a profusion of light and turquoises are characteristic of the Tver school.

It was in the XIVth century that Moscow began to develop rapidly and dragged the other Russian states into the struggle with the Tartars. After the victory of Koulikovo in 1380, the Moscow princes assumed control of the nationalist movement to free Russia from Mongolian bondage. Their court became a centre of attraction for painters and craftsmen from the other principalities. It was likewise in Moscow that the artists from southern

Slav countries invaded by the Turks sought refuge. Relations with Byzantium, broken off at the time of the Tartar incursions, were resumed. Thus in 1344 the Metropolitan Theognoste was able to ask Greek masters to decorate his cathedral with frescoes. Some time before 1395 the famous Theophanes the Greek, who had already worked in Novgorod and Nijni Novgorod, arrived in Moscow. Furthermore we know that Moscow possessed many icons and devotional objects of Byzantine origin.

To begin with, the Moscow painters followed the Vladimir-Suzdal school, as may be seen by the superb icon of *St Boris and St Gleb* (Pl. 18), supposedly by a Moscow painter. These saints were the object of a widespread cult. Facing the spectator, they are shown in hieratic posture, dressed in tunics and mantles and wearing princely toques edged with fur. The cross each holds in his right hand reminds us that they died a martyr's death, the sword in the left hand that they were revered as the patron saints of princes and warriors. The rather heavy proportions and stiff postures associate this icon with those of the xiiith century. Moscow was later to borrow extensively from the rather original Byzantine art of the time of the Paleologues (Pl. 21). But the Moscow painters were to transform it out of all recognition in the course of an evolution in which a painter of genius, Andrei Rublëv (circa 1360-70 - 1430), was to play a determining role.

With Theophanes the Greek, Rublëv was actually the creator of the Russian iconostasis as we now know it. In 1405, moreover, these two masters worked in collaboration at the Blagoveshchensky Cathedral in Moscow. They raised the height of the iconostasis so that it completely hid the altar from the congregation. The Byzantine iconostases were relatively low, being designed for a "deisis" of half-length figures, and the two rows of "local" or "occasional" icons. In Blagoveshchensky Cathedral Theophanes the Greek replaced these half-length figures by full-length figures of the *Virgin* (Pl. 19) and *St Michael the Archangel*

17

The Ascension (detail). Moscow School. Second quarter of fifteenth century. Tretyakov Gallery, Moscow.

The Dormition of the Virgin (detail). Tver School. (See Plate 17).

(Pl. 20), increasing the height of the icons to more than six feet. Rublëv followed his example: three years later he was to paint icons nearly ten feet high for the Cathedral of the Assumption. Thus extended, the iconostasis acquired new artistic significance. What was originally just a partition took on the proportions of a wall hung with several rows of large icons. To the traditional series were added those of the Prophets, the Patriarchs, and so on. All this constituted a monumental ensemble without precedent in Byzantium or elsewhere. Russia is rich in forests and the painters were not sparing of wood. So the iconostasis, which functioned as a support for a great many evangelical and hagiographic scenes, replaced mural painting to some extent.

Most of the icons we admire in museums as works of art in their own right were originally integral parts of a large ensemble, the iconostasis. The latter having fundamentally an architectural construction, the painter was obliged to simplify forms, lines and volumes so that they would be seen better at a distance. In this way the iconostasis contributed to the formation of that concise, unencumbered style so typical of the best xvth century icons.

A characteristic luminosity and an exceptional richness of feeling distinguish the works attributed to Rublëv (Pl. 22, 23 and 25). Rublëv's saints are inspired by his own conception of moral perfection; generous to a degree, they are ever ready to help. These images move us by their purity and poetry even today.

The *Trinity* (Pl. 25) is the most celebrated work of Rublëv. According to chronicles, this icon was painted in memory of Sergei of Radonezh, well-known founder of the Trinity monastery. The angels, seated at a low table, form such a closely-knit group that it is impossible not to interpret it as embodying the ideal of peace and harmony. The whole composition revolves around the chalice. The angels on the left and in the centre are blessing it. Their attitude is the key which enables us to interpret the complex symbolism of the picture. The angel in the centre represents Christ. Thoughtful, with head bent to the left, he blesses the chalice, thus indicating that he is prepared to offer himself as a sacrifice. God the Father (the angel on the left), whose face expresses profound grief, is encouraging him in his sublime gesture. The angel on the right represents the power of the Holy Ghost. We have here the embodiment of the greatest sacrifice of which love is capable (a father commits his son to death). But the artist goes even further: he shows the act of submission, the son accepting.

In Rublëv's *Trinity*, as in all great works, composition, colour and line rhythms obey a guiding principle. The angels, almost ethereal in their lightness and grace, are so placed around the table that they form a circle. The circle theme may be regarded as the key to the whole composition. It is evident in the central angel's head, turned leftwards, in the way the two seats are brought together, in the curve outlining the angel on the right, in the contours of mountain and tree. Less emphatic than the Italian "tondi", the circle theme here vibrates softly and discreetly. The painter has no fear of breaking the circular rhythm by introducing a vertical portico: he know his composition will gain in freedom and elasticity. The turn of the central angel's head, which disturbs the symmetry of the upper part of the picture, does not worry the painter, who merely moves the seat to the right to restore the balance. The chalice, too, instead of occupying the centre of the table, is placed to the right, where it balances the central angel's left-turned head. This liberal use of deliberate asymmetry gives the composition a remarkably open feeling. While the volumes remain centred and balanced, the composition acquires complexity as a result of the many variations on the circle theme. By fitting the composition into a simple geometrical figure, the circle, Rublëv restricts it almost entirely to the two-dimensional plane of the panel on which the icon is painted. And although the angels on either side are seated in front of the table and the central angel at the back, they appear to be on the same plane. Extremely slight, the depth is in strict correlation to the height and width of the panel. The three dimensions are thus in harmony, making of Rublëv's icon a perfect work of art. By excluding relief and using line and colour as his sole means of expression, Rublëv succeeded in preserving the two-dimensional rhythm which has always attracted Russian painters and which endows their compositions with surprising airiness.

Perhaps the most remarkable thing about this icon is the colour. Closely bound up with the design, it is the essential factor in the artistic quality of an icon distinguished by its harmony, clarity and purity. The colour range of the *Trinity* expresses with rare eloquence the idea of concord between the three angels.

A characteristic of Rublëv's art is the almost total absence of shadow. If the painter introduces a dark patch or a deeper tone it is solely to bring out the luminosity of another colour. This clever handling of colour gives Rublëv's palette its extreme luminosity and also an exceptional transparency reminiscent of Piero della Francesca. By skilfully combining three shades of blue Rublëv produces subtle harmonies with complex overtones. The visitor, on leaving the room where the *Trinity* is shown, cannot easily forget the resonance of these extraordinary colours.

With Rublëv's works the Russian art of the icon reached its peak. But Rublëv was not the only great master. Many talented painters were working around the same period (the end of the xivth - the beginning of the xvth century) and they did not all belong to the same school. Though icons of the Moscow school, such as the *Nativity* (Pl. 24), clearly reflect Rublëv's influence, the hagiographic icon of *St Michael the Archangel* (Pl. 26) reveals the hand of an independent painter. The upheld sword, the

St. Michael the Archangel (detail). Moscow School. (See Plate 26).

hard, stern face, give the Archangel such a warlike air that one can almost hear the bugles sounding.

Another unparalleled master was produced by the Moscow school in the xvth century - Dionisii (circa 1440-1508). He comes within the Rublëv tradition. Tendencies which were to develop from the middle of the xvth century on are evident here: a more profane treatment of religious themes, drawing for its own sake, chromatic effects, miniature-like delicacy in the modelling of the faces.

Clearly Dionisii strove to maintain the spirituality and the purity of Rublëv's art (Pl. 27 and 28). He too was fond of light, gay colours and generous line harmonies. Some new features are nevertheless discernable in his art: the faces of the saints no longer express the same strength of feeling; the colours have lost in vigour, and the artist seems to prefer washed-out tones and compositions with an abundance of ornamental motifs. With his more profane conception of the religious picture Dionisii favours the graceful, elegant and delicate. His work further reflects the growing importance of aesthetic canons and norms, auguring a more and more conventional art. Thus the art forms of the xvth century, which were to open a new era in Russian painting, imperceptibly took shape.

The great period of the icon coincides with Masaccio's reform in Italy and the painting of the Ghent altarpiece by the Van Eyck brothers in the Netherlands. The powerful current of the Renaissance, which swept over most of Europe, did not reach Russia. It would therefore be a mistake to study Russian art within the framework of Renaissance realism. The universe created by these early Russian painters requires very different criteria. Then and then alone may we feel the full impact of its spiritual wealth and of its perfect forms of expression.

ILLUSTRATIONS

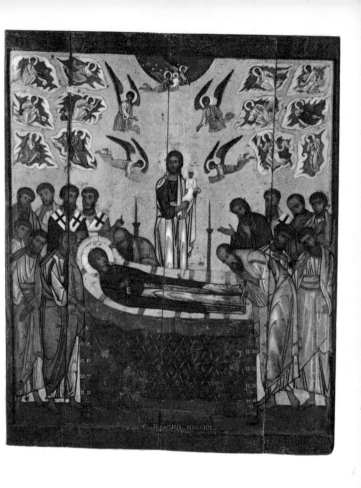

6

11

12

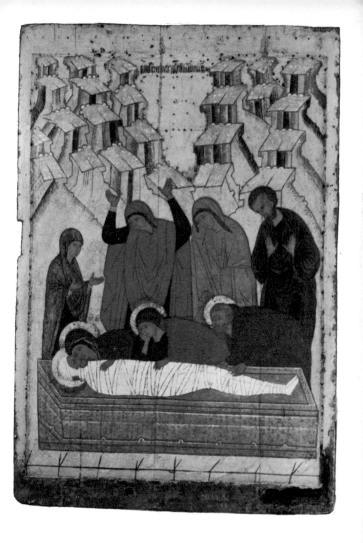

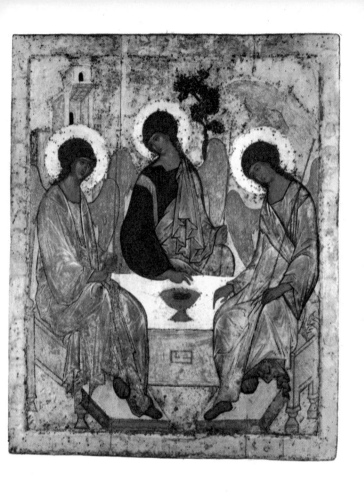

ОА АЛЕѮИ   УⷩꙀОРΕ

27

CONTENTS

CONTENTS

BIBLIOGRAPHY

N. Lihatčev, *Materialy dlja istorii russkogo ikonopisanija*, I-II, St. Petersburg, 1908-1910.

N. Ščekotov, *Nekotorye čerty stilja russkih ikon* XV *veka*, in "Starye gody" 1913, April, pp. 31-38.

"Russkaja ikona", I-III, St. Petersburg, 1914.

P. Muratov, *Drevnorusskaja ikonopis'*, J. S. Ostrouhov collection, Moscow, 1914.

P. Muratov, *Russkaja živopis' do serediny* XVII *veka*, in J. Grabar, "Istorija russkogo iskusstva", VI, Moscow, 1915.

G. Žydkov, *Moskovskaja živopis' serediny* XIV *veka*, Moscow, 1928.

N. Kondakov, *Russkaja ikona*, I-III, Prague, 1928-1934.

V. Lazarev, *Iskusstvo Novgoroda*, Moscow, 1947.

V. Lazarev, *Živopis' i skul'ptura Kievskej Russii; Živopis' i skul'ptura Novgoroda; Živopis' i skul'ptura Velikoknjažeskoj Moskvy; Dionisii i ego škola*, in "Istorija russkogo iskusstva", ed. I. E. Grabar', V. S. Kemenov, V. N. Lazarev, I-III, Moscow, 1952-1955.

USSR, *Early Russian icons*. Preface Igor Grabar, Texts Victor Lasareff and Otto Demus, Unesco World Art Series, 1958.

V. Lazarev, *Andrej Rublëv*, Moscow, 1960.